How we are loved

a spiritual odyssey

Carla Martin-Wood

Cover photography, ©2012, Randall J. Scholten

Fortunate Childe Publications
2012

With Gratitude

Fortunate Childe Publications thanks Randall J. Scholten for his generosity in allowing us to use his photograph, *The Gift*, for the cover of this book.

We encourage those who enjoy photography and appreciate the wonders of nature interpreted through the eye of a true artist to visit his website thedailysunset.com. Randall J. Scholten's work is available for purchase on Red Bubble (redbubble.com)

This book was written with love

For all those who wander and wonder,
who dare to question and explore;

For my son Zachary, who believes in science and logic,
and his mother, who believes in art and myth;

For Leslie, who lives her faith with a compassionate heart;

And for all my sisters in the dark craft of poetry:
Brenda, Joanne, Leena, Lise, Margot, Sally, and Wendy.

The Poems

I Ticking

II Olde tyme religion

The Poems

III How we are loved

All that is gold does not glitter,
Not all those who wander are lost.
J.R.R. Tolkien

Preface

... and there among my sisters wild and wise
in mists that robed a thousand ancient trees
I, too, took up my rattles and my drum ...
(from *Infidel*)

This eclectic collection embraces far more than rattling and drumming. With cadenced language that alternately screams, murmurs and sings, Carla Martin-Wood has shaped a most remarkable cosmos. Therein, we are not only asked to confront the darkest aspects of ourselves, but also to rejoice in the wider creation that she has set before us. The poet reveals how illumination can fill us if we but let it in. Her landscape has been formed under the hands of a dual deity, both harsh and generous, whose feminine aspect is particularly significant. It becomes a place where unanticipated miracles oppose unforgivable wrongs. Either extreme, the author seems to suggest, is crucial to our spiritual and moral progress as imperfect citizens of earth.

... we weeping kneel, as every memory
of that manmade hollow world
from which we came crumbles, dies,
and blissful, fades away.
(from *The Beautiful*)

Reading these poems will, indeed, evoke both tears and awe. It is impossible to encounter the Virgin Mary of *Holy Night* without a shiver of recognition; we appreciate her individuality even as we realize her connection to other lives, through endless generations.

No one can come away from *How we are loved* or *Praisepoem* without marveling at the author's insight. Her vision embraces every boon, broken hope, bright or shadowed being that leaps or flies or darts through water.

In other works, archetypal roots underlie actual as well as fictional events, some drawn from Martin-Wood's personal history. We rediscover familiar ideas and characters that "stroke myth into reality" wearing fresh guise. Eden's metaphorical apple is translated into time, faith, the planet itself. A dismembered woman is stitched together, Osiris-like, for proper burial. Rose, thorn and lamb are given fresh meaning in unexpected context. Though startled, we still understand.

Keep this volume on your nightstand. You will be revisiting it often.

Brenda Levy Tate

Author of *Wingflash* (The Pink Petticoat Press, 2011), *Cleansing* (Rising Tide Press, 2005) and *Beeline* (Lopside Press, 2007), and included in *Jailbreaks: 99 Canadian Sonnets* (Biblioasis 2008), an anthology of the editors' favorite Canadian sonnets of the past century.

I

Ticking

Ticking

Whatever staves off thoughts of death
that sits inside everything,
worm in apple,
hardcoded in DNA,
and counts down in whispers
that rasp, rattle, remind,
here in darkness where sleep eludes,

Whatever staves that off, we do –
booze or sex or new red stilettos –
whatever works to drown out
the dooming racket.

Tonight it's that sycamore
outside my bedroom window
when I was seven –
how it held the fat pearl moon
trapped in a net of twigs,
How homeland security
was downstairs baking brownies,
and spectral curtains floated gossamer,
while wind and branches wrote my future
in shifting hieroglyphs across the wall.

Diversionary tactics never work for long –
the old death-rattled whispers return to interrupt,
and sober mind's eye reads
those wall-written prophecies again,
knows my soul weighed and wanting.

Unfulfilled, unraveled, undone,
those early divinations of wind and tree,

so hopeful and pristine –
before the serpent swallowed the garden
put death into everything
set it ticking.

Contemplation after midnight

Doubt sits coiled
faith's appleworm
happy to sleep through
youth unconsidered
middle age unnoticed
bides its time till encroaching
death wakens it ravenous
and it begins to feed
upon the luscious fruit
to shrivel firm skin
till all is soft within
and no philosophy
will plump it back
restore the pristine
state of grace
when faith was new
unquestioned.

This apple Earth

spins sweet to its core, or so it seems
and whoever watches from the indifferent sky
oblivious as stone
sees no bruises
does not notice
how it has gone to seed these millennia
how it decays inside-out
sees only that morning and evening
of sixth-day perfection
when *it was very good*
cares not that it over-ripened
and quickly fell
inviting that irresistible
first-bite-yield-to-temptation
by rodent without and worm within
nor how it is scarred now
and bruised
softening inward
shrinking toward
the inevitable.

Vespers

Twilight lets fall its gossamer shawl
of indigo and awakening stars;
it floats down soft, swathes the valley,
tucked in for the night below,
and I am alone with You.

Questions whisper themselves,
my mind a beehive,
as I, Your errant stepchild,
the one who dares
open my heart to You, trusting,
place it into Your un-
trustworthy hand,
for none has wounded me more.

I speak to that Silence
beyond stones and older, ask once more
why You feed with hunger,
why You give only to snatch away,
why You countenance the rape of children,
why You bless and curse with selfsame Hand,
why You return abandonment for devotion.

From the valley, an owl's cry,
from the crest above, a flutter,
as raven scatters night with blacker wings
and this is all the Silence answers.

I am a better parent than You
I shout into echoing hills,

then tremble,
knowing I have heard the truth.

Beslan Fields
For Zhenia

I: Waiting Fields

In Beslan
a small boy trudges along
the edges of summer
seeing the field
he raced through
heedless of time
that sped by
faster than he

But school is inevitable
and he is eager
to join his friends
to learn
grow up
and maybe fly
beyond the stars
a cosmonaut
a member of Parliament
another Pushkin

It is not as though
summer will not come again
it waits in the fields forever.

II: Lesson in Russian

It is First September
the Day of Knowledge
a day of celebration

Beslan's children
dress in their finest
and faces shining
march eagerly to class

There is no regret
for summer fields lost
to winter learning

Self-conscious
they giggle and mug
for video cameras
file into the building
unaware
of the change in curriculum

The evening news reveals
a sinister show and tell
stricken pallor
eyes glazed
bewildered

Across the world
transfixed
we watch
doomed faces
fragile and familiar
as photographs of
Auschwitz or Rwanda

Outside
the army holds its fire
families agonize
long to comfort
touch
shelter what cannot be saved

Caught in the crosshairs
of a crescent moon
innocence falls again
days crawl and
let drag the heavy cross
till flesh is torn
the beast fed
and two gods
turn away as one.

III: The Grandmother

It is September in Beslan
and another child
is gently lowered
into the earth
of a field
that might otherwise grow wildflowers
or sleep silent under Russian snows

But this field must bear the burden
of so many children
who might have played in such a field
so many slack, small bodies
bearing their rootless dreams
into the dust

What songs this child sang
what graceless dance
what endearing word
what tangled curls

This small, tragic identity
blurs in the world's great grief
and is lost to the common field

But this grandmother knows
a room in her soul
now empty
oblivious to the watching world
she staggers, falls
knees buckle to earth
primal sound of grief
shatters heaven as
her hands fly to her face
fingers claw
fragile skin
blood
tears
mingle
fall
into the grave
with her beloved

whose wayward curls
she brushed and braided
whose song she heard
whose dance
whose unforgettable word
she knows.

Taking it all back

Heading south on 65,
passing the exit marked St. Joseph's Academy,
God, I remember that late October afternoon,
driving under the influence of guilt,
having forgotten it was my day to pick up the kids.

I remember how I begged Your forgiveness.

I'd spent the whole afternoon having a pedicure
before I remembered.
Now, hot pink toes peeked selfishly from sandals,
as I floored the gas pedal, flying down old 65,
imagining every pedophile and kidnapper,
every harm that could come to a pretty third grader,
standing on the curbside a whole hour alone,
believing I'd forgotten, didn't love her.

I remember how I craved absolution,
how I couldn't bear that I'd forgotten my child,
how dreams followed for months,
how still, the memory stings my eyes,
even though I found her having tea at the convent
laughing with Sister Maura, safe as houses.

Now, just before that turnoff, the radio blasts
recorded screams of 41 toddlers in Mexico,
as they burned alive in a daycare.

So about that time I begged Your forgiveness, God,
for being one hour late to pick up my child –
I take it all back.

Waiting Room

The dark-haired girl with the iPod hopes
Billie Holiday's slow-moaning blues will drown
the unwanted chatter of a man
who's been annoying her for hours,

while he turns his attentions to a nearby blonde,
who texts her aunt to return a library book,

and down the aisle, a boy holds his weeping mother,
promises he'll see her soon, takes the rosary pressed upon him,

while next to him, a woman wonders if you can go to hell
having an aged cat put down just so you can go to Europe,
remembers how the poor thing never saw it coming,
didn't even flinch when the vet slipped the needle in,

and across the aisle, the tough guy with a bold tattoo
remembers the lemon-scented hair of his wife,
who will be there waving when he arrives,

while a man dressed in Armani lies flawlessly
to a bluejeaned brunette, and a woman by the window
calls her secretary to complain about flight arrangements,
as a little boy sticks chewing gum beneath his seat,
and in the distance a baby gurgles, sucks a comforting thumb,

white noise of human hum and drum,
weightless conversation,
broken only by the loudspeaker:
Air France 447 to Paris now boarding.

*On June 1, 2009, 228 souls went down, lost on AF447, Paris bound from Rio. This poem is not intended to depict any actual person living or dead. Each is an individual loss that someone is grieving. May they rest in peace, and may their loved ones find solace.

Retribution

In a church that reeked
of dinner-on-the-ground potato salad
and Southern fried hypocrisy,
she shrieked at me, so everyone would hear

God's gonna strike you dead, you bitch!
Gonna reach down from heaven
and strike you dead!

Her self-righteous curse
because I dared step my peep-toe stilettos
onto her God's stomping ground.

I'd watched her grow up,
knew her summer lightning ways,
a gully washer of words
flash-flooded from her mouth,

with no take-backs ever,
the stubborn way she clung to ignorance
like a tenet of faith.

Weeks later, she surprised me in a parking lot,
begged my forgiveness,
seemed to astonish even herself
with such unfamiliar behavior.

I won't forget
how the tension in her body released
like a child limp with sleep
when we embraced –

out of character
as the chill that rode in on the hot breath of August.

That next spring spawned an F5 tornado,
and she was gone,
snatched away forever into a black sky
with her husband, their sons,
and a twisted faith
known only to snake handlers, holy rollers,
and speakers in tongues.

They hadn't even taken shelter.

Seeing her in that coffin, hands scraped and bruised,
I kept thinking how her cuticles needed tending,
how dirty her nails were,
wondered how they got that way,
what rough and unforgiving thing she had clung to,
borne skyward, flung earthward, without a prayer,
dismembered, stitched back together for burial.

Not privy to our parking lot reconciliation,
her redneck relations cut a wide and fearful swath
around me after that,
whispered whether I had my own slave-god
to do my bidding,
riding down through thunderheads of reckoning,
hurling hot bolts of judgment
at God-fearing folk,

reaching down through the whirlwind,
taking retribution.

*This poem is not intended to depict any actual person living or dead, and
any similarity is strictly coincidental.*

Saint Sharon

She stands on the corner
across from Calvary Baptist Church.

Parents shield children's eyes from
her body skeletal, draped in rags,
covered with sores,
infested with god-knows-what,
holding aloft a bible,
pages rat-gnawed and stained,
cover soaked in piss
from the puddle that pooled unnoticed
as she slept
in the alley last night.

She stands in her filth and sermonizes
Who do men say that I am?
You will deny me.
Can you love me when I look like this?
Do you love me?

Lost boy

Wholesale warehouse
Saturday morning
carts loaded
with obscene quantities of things
people don't use
buy to save money
shoppers check lists
cell phones to ears
oblivious to the lost

boy almost transparent
wedged between
shelves of cinnamon
from Saigon and
stacks of Persian rugs

six-year old legs
scrawny
scarred
half-hidden face reveals
one eye dark
as chocolate from Côte d'Ivoire
wide and deep as a gulf
tears well/ spill/ dry
on dusty cheeks
his face a battlefield
where everything is

Lost boy
loudspeaker shrieks

Where's your Mommy, little boy
the clerk demands loudly

leans into his face
offers a lollypop
a bright balloon
boy shrinks away
clerk shrugs
smacks bubblegum
winks at cashier
goes to talk

as the boy blends into cinnamon
does a chameleon fade
into multicolored rugs
leaves nothing visible

no one saw him go
final glance defiant
fist clenched
mouth screaming
silent.

Illumination

Late Louisiana afternoon
smell of gumbo mixes with pot
burdens heavy August humid air
sonofagun gonna have big fun on de bayou
some redneck white woman squawls
backed up by fiddle music
as

Modreen sits on the front stoop
blows downward into sweaty cleavage
trying to cool off
hair damp
dress sticking to her back
she bounces her fat lovechild
and prays for an unbiased world
some place where people look deep
some place with a breeze
some place not here
sits there till the sun goes down
when

their glow dulled
by the plastered wings
of a thousand doomed insects
street lights illuminate
a dead end street.

The Stone Girl

In a local churchyard, there stands an old statue. A little girl runs, a look of mild surprise on her face, six pennies embedded in her palm. She died in 1950, and this poem is based on the story people still share hereabouts.

Carnival on wheels
the ice cream lady approaches
hair coiled
serpentine
calliope music
blasting its siren call
to every child

Marisol jumps rope
life cartwheels inside her
she is perpetual joy
singing her five years
of olly-olly-oxenfree
Marco
Polo
red rover red rover
send Marisol over
ring around the roses
I'm a little Dutch girl
dressed in blue
all fall

down the drive she runs
Nonna! Ice cream!

Nonna presses six pennies
into her eager palm
and Marisol scatters
like blossoms

like butterflies
running toward
ice cream
and the lady
with sinuous hair
who beckons
between the old blue Studebaker
and Mr. Cannon's Oldsmobile

and then
(incomprehensible)
it is Breugel's *Icarus*
the world just going on
like it's nothing extraordinary
as a wingless child
takes flight
while Mrs. Rosario tends her garden
and Mr. O'Malley complains

Marisol rises
in slow motion
like a silent movie
but in heartstopping reality
a scream of tires
the sudden fall
of a child with coins to spend

empty sandals
on the pavement
as though they wait
for her to put them on again

Marisol barefoot and silent
sprawled on the newly watered grass
of Mr. O'Malley's front yard

coins still clenched
eyes wide with surprise.

she lies in the family plot
where Uncle Tito
who sculpted gravestones
created an everlasting tribute

The Stone Girl
we've come to call her
six pennies embedded
in her marble palm
eyes crinkled in laughter
always running
toward the lady
with serpentine curls
who beckons
and the calliope music
of an ice cream truck
blasting its siren call.

Sam

Always a grin
eyes cornflower bright
he ransacks garbage
behind the fast food place
harvests half a burger
morsel of fried pie
slower than he used to be
hopes they don't catch him
but easily distracted
spies a jonquil
cocks it behind one ear
winks at the rising sun

a mockingbird sings
the thousand faces of God.

Sunday in Wonderland

It's a beautiful day
Whoever-you-are
God or Allah or Gaia
a beautiful day in Wonderland
blue and gold and crisp
the polar cap hasn't melted yet
on good days
we still see the sun
it's a beautiful day indeed.

If you haven't noticed
we're civilized
it only required a few changes
instead of carnage in our wars
we rack up casualties
we televise beheadings now
in glorious HD
then run to send the video
to every single soul we know
and somewhere around old Eden
are pockets of genocide
but they're so easy to ignore
like a small leak in the basement.

It's a beautiful day
Whoever-you-are
Sacred Alien or Disney
whoever made this wonderful place
from intergalactic
mold and must
or ever so elegant fairy dust.

Seasons come and go
we still trust
the maples will manage a red in fall
and sometime near the Solstice
the yearly call
for peace on earth rings out
the crocus staggers up each spring
in perennial yellow and blue
and breaking through the crusted snow
it feigns a lesson or two
but we forgot so long ago
to listen.

It's a beautiful day
Whoever-you-are
wherever you went
wherever you hide
it's a beautiful day in the test tube here
and we all sing *Alleluia*
it's a beautiful day in the neighborhood
and we feel obliged to salute you.

Hummingbirds

How in the dapple shadowed early morning,
I fed you summerlong,
applauded every acrobatic flight,
held close each tender trust,
an unsuspecting Eve.

Darwin on Galápagos
would have guessed your family tree,
would have seen what I did not till now.

Disturbing, this resemblance,
feather to scale, needle beak to fang –
how aeons changed you not entirely,
made miniscule your form
and full of grace your aerial ballet,
how jeweled your glistering wings
ignite in early autumn's embered light,
disguise not quite the legacy of iridescent scale –
how ineffable whirr of hovering wings
cannot masque the doomed Edenic hiss.

We all have relatives we'd just as soon forget;
if you forgive my distant kin's neanderthalic ways –
Himmlers, Oppenheimers, and the rest –
I must forgive the serpentine in you.

I shall politely keep our small charade,
pretend I do not know your heritage,
and come next spring, shall fill this font again
with nectar-sweet delight –
fit only for the likes of God and you.

Redheaded Stepchild

It's me
your redheaded stepchild
the one who's been
staring at your Divine Backside
these five years

it's me wondering why
wondering what I did

did I sing out of tune
in choir or pronounce
your most-forbidden name

did I misspeak in one of those
poems I used to write for you

did I made a misstep when
I was trying to follow
one of those obstacle courses
you set up
predestined to fail

I have to wonder what I did
that was bad enough
to lose everyone
who mattered

I'm not Job
but I'm not Judas either
and if this is how you treat
your kids
then human and frail
I'm the better parent

They say
a stone was rolled
away from your tomb
and you stepped out
clean as a whistle
white as a lily

I'd like to believe that
again
like to stand with the righteous
and sing alleluia
but it's me
and I'm your redheaded stepchild
tugging at your sleeve
with my questions.

Leaving Santa

In those lost days
I snuggled safe
in Your Santa lap
never thinking
lulled into believing
that as long as I did
the right thing
I'd be saved
and secure

meanwhile
kids were taking it up the arse
from fathers in and out of habit
Your right hand men
and left hand pedophiles

meanwhile
wives were battered
elderly went homeless
poor went hungry
moguls daily raped the earth
dined on delicacies of fetal fingers
and hummingbird wings

meanwhile
animals were slaughtered
for skins to drape Hollywood
while the future
was shooting up in the alley
or shooting up high schools

meanwhile
Auschwitz
Oppenheimer's toy
Rwanda
Darfur
wars fought to line pockets

and I remembered
I had climbed
into Your cozy Santa lap
to escape obvious questions
like *Why?*
and I understood
that Free Will is the ultimate cop-out

just at that
righteous moment
when I felt
like that kid in the movie
who wanted a bb-gun
out came Your Big Boot
to my backside
and down the long slide
I flew.

Garden of Regret

There is the garden where nothing grows

where angels long ago
doused flaming swords
and walked away like men do
at quitting time

once free
no one wishes
to find this place again

where no merciful snow
falls to camouflage
with blind innocence
the disillusion
of dissolution

this garden of
perpetual winter
where no thorn
wounds
and no herb
heals
where no god walks
lonely in the evening
looking for conversation

and the green bewildered
serpent coils languid
about the wasted fruit.

War and peace

After my Black Ops daughters
ripped through with AK-47s
plundered remains
scorched earth
closed the door

After the covert companion
stealthed in my DNA
made itself known
sunk teeth
into bones
began to chew

I moved into a one bedroom flat
with no windows
and a coffee pot for one
forgot how to dust
stopped planting things
learned that recycled photographs
make good kindling
bought a goldfish named Sushi
and with no one dragging at my skirts
finally had time to read Hardy
not at all the pessimist
I'd heard about.

Stained

glass
steel
summit of faith
those full of grace gather
drugged on opiate religion
following collective unconscious

Kýrie, eléison

outside
the filthiest alleyway blossoms
bedraggled earth renews
inside
stations of my cross
pretzel-twisted legs
knees that do not bend
back that does not bow
burdens I've dragged
into a building hopelessly
stained

Christé, eléison

glass Queen of Heaven
starlit and crowned
light filters through
crystalline pure
she stands robed
in everlasting virginity
upon her crescent
but never looks my way

Kýrie, eléison

angels leaded and stained
tender or angry
or rushing off to kill firstborns
no guardians dear
they overlook me
like a bloody doorpost

Agnus dei

I could wish to believe
but I know
incense manipulates
like pot in an elevator
everyone gets stoned

you take away the sins of the world

tsunami them fathoms deep
bury them under earthquake rubble
cast them into bottomless pits
turn them to salt
how many Isaacs slaughtered
how much more must you take away

the sins

I cannot reconcile
your abandonment
father of perpetual pain
I cannot forgive
false advertising
love promised
peace offered
stained

the sins

glass effigy
on its Tiffany splendored cross
as if that were enough
its sorrowful eyes
look straight
at me craving
absolution

eléison.

II

Olde tyme religion

Restless

I have a need to go
far from the mongering throng
from Wall Street wolves
and silver-spooned entitled
from that place
where bodies of unfortunates
form ladders to climb to the top

I have a need to go
to wilderness that claims no boundaries
where valleys stretch and yawn
their way to evening
where singsong cicadas
welcome in the moon
and long-fingered rivers
meander metallic and aimless
through momentary shades of blue
that settle and deepen
into night
and there
I have a need to stay.

How I left

Even as chameleon twilight abandons
the heavens in shades of rose
that subtle shift
to lavender, then grey
so that one hardly notices
when night has fallen
even as mountain shadows
swallow the valley
losing limpid light
to gradual darkness
even as everything touched
is changed forever
fruit bruised, petal wilted
even as wonder fades from eyes
now jaded and hard
even as stone splits asunder
over years of winter
freezing and melting
with perennial brutality

even as a neglected child may wade
too far from safely shallow
may step from the fatal underwater shelf
and disappear.

Apostasy
for Riqué

Take off your robes, Father
and wear instead the habit
of your youth
before you became
the retina of the world
deciding which images
receive your holy imprimatur

for I recall
long, libidinous Tuesday night tangos
on a roof near Washington Square
and Friday evenings
that brimmed with cheap red wine
and midnight conversation
at a dusty place in Chelsea
where the only Host was named Sergé
where you smoked Turkish cigarettes
flicking the ashes
as you spoke in half-drunk tongues
of poetry and jazz
till the numbness left
and so did we

today I found a relic, Father
your glove
still smelling of leather and smoke
still tucked in the pocket
of my old coat

now I find what passes for you here
passion contained

will confined
and I cannot believe
till I thrust my hand
into whatever wound you bear

so take off your robes, Father.

womanpoem

There was a woman at the edge of the forest
and she was singing songs
she was singing songs
to the earth that opened itself to bring forth life
as she did
songs
to the moon that waxed and waned in its cycle
as she did
songs
to the waters that ebbed, that flowed
as she did
and she sang down fire
she sang the winds from their four towers
she sang till the earth quickened
beneath her dancing feet
and water poured forth from the listening stones
and something older than morning
heard

and something was borning
in the burning shadows
in the singing silence that fell between her words
in the dawning of that darkness

There was a woman at the edge of the forest
and she was calling down power
she was calling down power
from the womangods
power
in all its ancient names
Ishtar, Isis, Demeter, Hecate
power

calling on chaos to bring the order
power
calling on madness to give birth to reason
power
till the scales could balance once more
and something older than sunrise
heard its unspeakable name

There was a woman at the edge of the forest
and she was cursing the things
that blackened the soul of earth
cursing
war and avarice and violence
cursing
marketplace manlogic
cursing
the rape of the Mother
and she was invoking
an older order
a wiser way
a womanpath

and something was borning
in the burning shadows
in the singing silence that fell between her words
in the dawning of that darkness

There was a woman at the edge of the forest
and she was weaving womanstories
she was weaving womanstories
like spiderwebs
and the light fell clinging silver to her words
stories
of the power of the daughters
who birthed and taught and nurtured men

men who ruled to ruin
stories of strength
stories of the source of all
of the daughters
of the Mother
abused
bruised
battered by the power of the manworld
which is brutality
which is war
which is the power of the marketplace
and something older than death
rose up angry

There was a woman at the edge of the forest
and she was singing down the power
she was naked
her hair was wild and singed
and she smelt of fire
because she had walked through the center
because no one circumnavigates hell
she had brought forth
pomegranates for the daughters
and laurels to crown them
and she had brought forth a new way
she told them of their Mother
and that their time is beginning

and something was borning
in the burning shadows
in the singing silence that fell between her words
in the dawning of that darkness

and something older than birth
opened its arms in welcome.

Into this Eden

Let me not go down
into the earth that bore me
let not flesh sink
to alabaster bone
in silence
darkness
and alone

Once within the Everglades
dazzled by gilded reeds
and dappled shade
beneath a bright
and cerulean sky
I watched
color and light
conspire as friends
to shift and part and suddenly
reveal a golden panther
in the splinter of a moment's end
then saw it just as quickly fade
to camouflage again

Let me go down so
myself disperse
meld into autumn light
merge and mingle
with shadows cast
by birds and dragonflies
let my words rise
a faint incense
upon the breeze
an almost-heard inflection

that sings hollow
rings of hope
within the sound
of water running softly underground

o let the meter that was mine
the living rhyme
that pumped my heart
and gave me life
and any worthy dream
I might have had
be one
with every glory burning bright
upon this earth

not high above
nor in between
nor yet below
but into this Eden
let me go
thus let me stay.

Windfall

Behind the hundred orchard rows,
where lithe-limbed trees
in sprayed and pruned perfection
lift tame treasures through mellow Indian Summer,
till fruit is finished, grown unblemished, red and round,
more suited for a photograph than eating,

Past tall grasses long ignored, spared by mowers,
where crickets harmonize at evening's edge,
where owl calls low as fireflies dim their lanterns
with the year's decline,

There, a vestige of the elder farm remains,
preceding advent of machine, relic of the days
when human hands took autumn fruit
as free as any Adam

Lone surviving tree, gnarled and ancient,
sequestered deep within concentric rings,
does something like a memory lie?

Tire swings that creaked
and spanned a score of summer lives,
suffering freckled Robin Hoods to pilfer her green fruit
and climb her patient ladders into manhood,
while shaded soft beneath her latticed boughs,
beguiled by flutter, butterfly and blossom,
drowsy maidens slumbered dreaming royals
sure to come.

Her ragged leaves stir,
just slightly tinged with russet,

arthritic limbs, twisted and determined
to hold with firm resolve her happy burden,
irregular and speckled ruby globes
grown pendulous, plumped, heavy honeyed,
waiting wayward child or hungry vagrant
to climb and claim her treasured harvest
autumnal and sweet.

Then comes a storm too bitter, unexpected,
and windfall apples cast a holy circle
of premature bounty.

Let us take this tempting orb before it spoils,
cut cross-wise, mark the story secreted within seeds
in poignant pattern, knowledge half-forgotten.
Behold the perfect pentacle, the core within the fruit –
air, fire, water, earth and Spirit,
the eternal equilibrium,
partnership of nature and divine.

Before the fall, before machine,
when human hands took autumn fruit
as free as any Adam.

*Kore's sacred fruit is the apple. When an apple is cut through its equator,
both halves will reveal a pentagram shape at the core, with each point on
the star containing a seed. Each point symbolic, respectively, of the
elements of nature and Spirit, the sum symbolizing the balance of the
Universe. The Roma call this core the Star of Knowledge.*

The Beautiful

Beyond the scope of dull mathematics,
pompous science, and other lies
we tell ourselves,
where the light bends at a sweeter slant,
and leads us down a strange familiar path,
into a hidden grove whose aged branches
vault toward the sky to paint their own Sistine,
sequestered in this peace, in simple grandeur,
cloistered here, we find at last

The Beautiful

never to be seen,
save by the random blessed,
we who dreamt too long
within a toadstool ring,
or careless stumbled on this place
world worn and weary,
soul chafed, wings clipped,
our native lustre tarnished,
and here like the fated knight
before La Belle Dame Sans Merci,
we weeping kneel, as every memory
of that manmade hollow world
from which we came crumbles, dies,
and blissful, fades away.

Infidel

The day my joints could no longer bend
to rest upon the kneeler
as I lip-synced words I was assured
the blest worldwide were mouthing at that moment

The day my muscles, wasting from disuse
could not bear the slightest bow before the altar
and I perceived the disapproving
stares of priest and congregation

The day I found the Host had lost its savor
and moneychangers ran a poser's show
to detriment of those
The Christ had come to serve

That day I left the bleak edifice
of iron and steel and glass erected
by man and rooted in man's words
to seek the place where women go

and there among my sisters wild and wise
in mists that robed a thousand ancient trees
I, too, took up my rattles and my drum
and let the rhythm of my blood
speak all my prayers
and all my hymns

I let the forest sing.

Olde Tyme Religion

It's in the mistletoe
felled by the golden sickle
gathered into the mantle of white

it's in the bark of the oak
and those ancient faces
hiding there, clear as carvings
when you half-close your eyes
and viscera recall
the double-helix memory

see how they watch you
as druid roots stir across millennia
weave about your mind
that's when you know

it's in the healing blood
of twin white bulls
spilt on the sixth night of the moon

it's recorded in the grain
whorled into circles
counted like sins
that need no confession
the poems they wrought
to hold their history
imprisoned in concentric rings

it's in the lingering smell
of sap like communion wine
so sweet you cease
cutting firewood to dry for winter

and lick its blood from your fingers
know the taste of something important
fermented but forgotten

and something in you longs
to raise a hymn to harvest
to air and fire, earth and water
to chant and dance
about the flames
to remember the Old Ones

listen — do you not hear them
in the rocking of your heart
in the pulse of your spirit?

Grace

for Leslie

When birds feel winter stirring in their bones,
they come to me for seed and suet and grain,
bits of berries, fruit, peanut butter
pressed in pine cones hung with bright ribbon.

Too cold to sit out on my porch,
it becomes an avian restaurant,
dishes hanging, seeds scattered,
things filter down,
chickadees and finches on the feeders,
cardinals and jays upon the floor.

I'll clean it up come spring,
but not before I've left enough
string and feathers, yarn and twigs
to help with April nesting.

Why this brings me joy, I cannot say.
I do not watch them, draw my blinds,
and let them live in peace,
in some small comfort without fear.

I never made up ten restricting rules with corollaries
and threats of eternal roasting on a spit,
if they fail to straighten up and fly right.
Nor do I peek into their nests
to ascertain if one has strayed
and found another's mate more pleasing.

Nor do I ask for a tenth
of whatever wage a sparrow earns,
or require that I be honored

on certain days of the week.

Nor do I demand confessions
and weigh their happy wings with heavy hearts,
nor yet prefer a redbird to a blue.

I do not know when one has fallen
prey to prowling cats, or when a boy steals
bright blue eggs to show at school,
(though I would stop him if I could).

Wren to oriole, they go their way unfettered,
and I go mine without a thought,
except that I fed something
beautiful.

Rite

In this circle of white stones
we stroke myth into reality
follow the path of the Old Ones
cast seeds in their season
measured by motion of stars
undulance of grasses
grown up around us
floats about our knees
as we move in tidal rhythm
dance to the sacred
sing to Mother Gaia
bare feet sense earth's pulse
cicadas chant at moonrise
welcome us
home.

Solstice Night

Now the long, slow tango between the dark and light,
as another year exhausts itself
and falls away to longest night.
Now the winds, loosed from their four towers,
conspire to bury in snow all things worth losing.

Old griefs, empty chairs,
joyless mornings, tattered faith –
we let them die, let them lie
beneath the icy crust.
When April brings the melt,
we'll hardly recognize them anymore.

For this, we trade gold and azure skies
for winter's grey and glower.
For this, we bear the numbing freeze,
for this, we share the weight
of burdened branches that snap and creak,
wet black bark, sharp against the dazzle.

Now counting stars, we watch,
faces pressed to the window,
where dancing flames reflect
and burn away the old
to forge the new.

On defying the natural order

In loving disagreement with Radcliffe Squires, Robert Frost and Gerard Manley Hopkins

If the light
in autumn's final leaf
did not fall
or fade
or sink
to grief
but danced
into winter
a solitary wonder

refused to grace
the forest floor
leafmeal there
and nothing more
unwithered
daring everything
the deadly frost
the shock of cold
could shake the blight
and still burn gold
without a flicker

if that light
held strong and knew
another spring
its sap renewed
in every vein
and summer, too

o, for such hope
in such a light

that never dimmed
but dared the night
rebuked for all
the killing child
whose arrogance
would force its fall
and take its place

o, such a light
so dark an art
could topple
Eden's applecart.

Warning

Don't get sidetracked by spring
whatever you do
don't look at that apple tree
flaunting her blossoms in the wind
shameless and out of control
shifting lace
abuzz and aflutter
coyly revealing limbs
anxious for fruit
type . . . anything
google obscure subjects
t3X7 y0uR fri3nd5 In L337 spe@K

whatever you do
don't enter that Garden
don't give yourself over to Beauty
she'll knock you to your knees
and there you'll be
sprawled on the path
with a goofy look on your face
like Paul on the road to Damascus
for the veil has been rent
and you've glimpsed
the Holy of Holies
and now you just aren't
with the program

people gather around you
dial 911
take photos with their cell phones
post your pathetic self on YouTube
facebook their friends
OMG OMG OMG

offer you bottled water
and a religious tract

while somewhere
hovering above your own body
you see
the Light within the light
and drink
the never bottled
pure unenhanced
completely unmessed with
living water
from the original well-
spring.

III

How we are loved

Psalm of the Lost Lamb

I seek you
as the blind wolf searches
the caverns of its inner darkness
for the moon
having sensed
the silver rising
and howling
knows within emptiness
the unseen more

I fear you as
the aspen leaf trembles
in late autumn sun
and knows not
which small breeze
will end its clinging
send it dying
to the forest floor

I thirst for you as
the parched earth splits open
cracks apart
in its agony of waiting
the quenching rain

I was alone
among the arrows of my enemies
I turned to find you
and you were gone
you abandoned me to my grief
and left me powerless in my agony
you stood apart

and permitted my flesh to be stripped
and my bones to be polished as jewels
to adorn those who despised me

O how I have hated you
in my sorrow
how I do not understand
your sublime treachery
how I cannot comprehend
your mysterious purpose
your oceanic absence

I am worn smooth
as the river stone
assaulted by rapids
these thousand years
no edges left
no fight left in me

You are the honey
hidden sweet
within the comb
covered by bees
that threaten
the intruder

You are the elusive nectar
deep within the throat
of the unblemished lily
attainable only by certain hummingbirds
and butterflies

I eat the bitter rind of despair
and wait for you in the
deserts of my longing

I am alone
as the vastness of space
as the infinite vacuum
between the stars

I am still
as the prey of the spider
wrapped in silken threads
and waiting for disaster

I am silent
as flightless birds
that have forgotten
how to sing

I am empty
as jars of clay
that once contained
the wine of a
lost civilization

O leave
the hundred others
and come
to find me.

The child who can believe

I want to be the child who can believe
and never watch the wonder die away
into the faded dawn of a graceless day

I want to be the child who always sees
the fairy in the dragonfly's disguise
the beauty in the beast that men despise

I want to be the child who still has faith
in Christmas night and early Easter morn
the triumph of the rose above the thorn

You may keep your science black and white
hypotheses, experiments alike
let reason give you comfort in the night

But leave to me the legend and the lore
and I will shelter them within my heart
that miracle and myth shall not depart

And I shall find my comfort in the word
that echoes down millennia to remind
that truth is in the heart and not the mind

I'll follow close that other child who leads
down twisted paths where only faith can go
to glories only innocence can know

I want to be the child who can believe
and never watch the wonder die away
into the faded dawn of a graceless day.

Holy night

. . . from henceforth all generations shall call me blessed. Luke 1:48

starshine

and they come
addled old men
freezing in cold desert night
lambs draped across their shoulders
to keep them warm
and maybe they wonder
if those were real angels
telling them to fear no harm
or just the madness that sets in
when it's only you
and the sheep for so long

and they come
the three we've heard about
stargazing men with funny names
we always forget
bringing wise gifts
of homage and worship and death
for the unlikely king
who sucks his thumb
and snuggles down to sleep
in the cow's trough

and the others
tinker and tailor and weary old sailor
tempestuous fisherman
town harlot
miller and vintner
butcher, baker, candlestick maker
tax collector

a man blinded by the Light
the adulteress
and her empty-handed accusers
rich man, poor man, beggar man, thief
the Centurion with his vinegar sponge
disillusioned Crusaders
the artist who paints the elaborate ceiling
a pope or two
the plain and the beautiful
doctor, lawyer, Indian Chief
the old lady whose social security check is late
crazy Joe who sleeps in the alley
the cheerleader who got knocked up
and her quarterback boyfriend
so many
frightened and hungry and homeless and sick

o – they are lined up
clear back to Rome
across massive mountains
and oceans
and millennia
from Bethlehem
though only
she can see them all
this doe-eyed teenager
with the sweet face
she who lies on coarse and bloody straw
her life interrupted
by a dove bearing mystery
who opened her womb
as she now opens her heart
with its many rooms
to all those people

lined up outside the stable
inviting them to enter in
and be warm

she who shivered in the cold
numbed by her own sweat
whose lung-bursting scream
split cold night air
as light split the heavens
when she pushed him forth
and he looked around
at all he'd made
and maybe wondered
why he had thought
it was so good
in the first place
but then curled up
against her breast
and fell to snoring

she watches
as they pay their respects
smile and coo at him
as though he were any baby
or simply kneel
so stricken
on this night

when anything can happen
this night of angels and doves
whose wings whisper
his name
and it echoes down centuries
like music
on this night

when we can say things like
Behold!
and *Gloria!*
and *Alleluia!*
and no one laughs
on this night
when there are lights
of every color
when we stroke the myth
or treasure the memory
whatever our belief

because the star faded
long ago
and the stable
fell to ruin
in the labyrinthine caverns
of history
but we took the mystery
and the wish
and the hope and peace and love
of that story
into our hearts
as the girl
took us into hers
on this night
this Holy Night.

Holy Night was nominated for The Pushcart Prize in 2010

Pockets

He wore a coat with many pockets
one held the gore and smoke of battlefields
another a meadow
where poppies burned scarlet
amongst gilded wheat

It was a coat with many pockets
one muffled the cries of children
lovers were hidden away in one
and in another
there was straw
a feeding trough
and a lot of good intentions

There were many pockets
one for babies orphaned or abandoned
another concealed barren women
several held broken promises
questions without answers
the futility of pain

How heavy, these many pockets
one bulged with forgotten gardens
seeds unplanted
oil-slicked waters
and air that corrodes

So many pockets
bloody altars in one
a crucifix rusted in another
there was a rosary strung with Stars of David
crescent moons and a pentagram

manmade stories
that lost more meaning
with every telling

A coat with many pockets
enough for the whole world
one for sins
another for good deeds
now that I remember
he stood a bit lop-sided

Burdened by so many pockets
with prayers and sunsets
and first stars rising
on nameless hopes

There were so many pockets
the addicted and estranged
empty hands of the hungry
the hollow-eyed homeless
with only this small pocket
for shelter

There were these many pockets
one for me
that I kept falling out of
climbing back up
by fraying threads
then sliding back down
as he trudged on
dragging the great coat behind him.

Don't doubt this spring

Don't doubt this spring.
Don't question the frost that clings to the tulip.
Be glad.
If the morning air breathes a warning,
ignore it.
It will go away.

I have spent the night
in the belly of the storm
where was no song
and no flower
but grief only
like an absence
of air.

Yet this dawn I swear
I see glory
and a flame rises
east of my soul
undefeated.

Sunrise

in the light that rises
victorious

over a dark world
mired in its hungers
blind of heart

where unwilling children begin
routines of breakfast
and flossing and trudging
to classrooms undesirable

as resentful workers commute
through cul de sac lives
from empty home
to mundane cubicle

and the retired faithful
kneel to worship self-
righteous beside the jaded
Sisters at early Mass

somewhere in that chaos
there is a singular moment
in an unremarkable life
when a heart beats
joyous at the butterfly effect
of quickening fetus

or a long-neglected spirit
faced with the elemental
testimonies of creation

revives in fresh assurance
of a grand design

or unexpected wonder
punctuates tears
as a friend crosses over
from pain to peace

in the light that rises
victorious.

For those who will not love

For those who will not love
a garden holds no torment
no tears wrung bloody from the thorn-pressed heart
no silver-bartered kiss
no hour of crosses goes burning in the skull
toward cock-crowed denial in the morning

for them
water remains water
wine remains wine

theirs is a loss of wonder

where no stones are rolled away
and sleep is undisturbed
eternal.

Blessing

In this forest where
vermilion autumn
burns to embers
yet another year
my boots have worn
a long accustomed path

I marked the berries
going red
the sorrel's tattered flame
and yet I failed
to see or take
good note of that
which startles now
and takes my breath
this morning

within a tiny clearing
visible just now
through thinning brush
this tree so
small and low and lit
by fleeting brilliance
of the rising sun
that turns to gold
with Midas beam
each slender branch

not leaf
nor bird

nor even bark
disturbs its spare design
nor mars
its pale and polished
limbs that lift
as to relinquish all
to heaven at last
in seeming praise
or longing

o make me thankful
for this gift
of emptiness
this gift of
light.

The gift

Inspired by the photography of Brenda Levy Tate & Randall Scholten

Gingerly stepping down ridges of shale
sharp-edged and slick with the first flakes of snow
beneath skies brooding heavy and dark
I made my way at sunrise
seeking the gifts I've come to know
wait for me at the tide's edge

shells opalescent and whorled
seaglass translucent as aquamarine
driftwood worn smooth by loving
of waves and salt and time

I never know just what I'll find

but there is this faithful knowledge
that something waits
beyond the jagged rise
something to pocket
and call my own
to place on a shelf
to remind
the journey is worth the dare
the rocks are worth the climb

and yet
today I found nothing
though I walked a mile or more
scavenging the water's edge
disappointed as a child
who wakes forgotten
Christmas morn

just as I had turned to go
empty-handed and bereft
a golden shaft of light broke through
and sweeping down in graceful arc
on pinions shining white
as any angel well might hope to wear
a gull swooped low
to skim the mirrored waves
and scatter light about me everywhere

there in its bright reflection
I knew myself rewarded for the climb
no beggar poet could have asked for more
than this simple, earthbound angel
bearing its golden tithe of heaven's store.

Ebb

The sea's long fingers
reach even these rocks
make tiny currents
in the wake of a withdrawn tide
trickle from ledges
drip into pools
make hollow music
flow back home
at ebb of day

the language of morning
is not spoken here
where gulls screech
irreverent vespers
and sandpipers
write vague prophecies
in hieroglyphs upon the shore
where the remnant sun goes down
a ginger stain
against the dusk
like a leak in the roof
of heaven

but as the darkness grows
brighter the lighthouse shines
its long, slow beacon
flashes hope
and points the way
for battered sailors
seeking morning.

Dark night

If you gaze for long into an abyss, the abyss gazes also into you.
Friedrich Nietzsche

Gazing into the abyss
finding the dark unexpected
stone cold stare returned
we startle

to see thriving in that rude landscape
marauding monsters
we believed we had unseated long ago
still mirrored in ourselves
we are stunned

to overhear our own voices
echo the unkind word
spread the virus of suspicion
cast a veil of evil nuance
upon another's hard-won reputation
we cringe

to know our dearth of tenderness
meshed with hell's own intention
a bitter root that anchors itself
deep into the most well-meaning soul
until we rise

and open a window into Light
to deep inhale
the morning's sweet and cleansing breath
to open ourselves
embrace the Glorious
hold fast the hallowed Presence
that withers what grows malignant
in the darkness.

How we are loved
1 John 4:16

What the river knows, it keeps
beneath ephemera of foam,
far below pull of eddies and currents,
beneath its bed
and into its cold dark heart,
though from the watershed
we can see

how it harbors fish and lamprey,
feeds swallow and raven,
slakes thirst of sheep and wolf,
all haphazard,

how it floods thirsty fields,
or careless withers into a parched arroyo,

how it goes where it wants,
demanding and turbulent,
carves through mountains,
erodes barren rock to fertile silt,

how it tumbles jagged stones
through rapids and waterfalls,
drags them indifferent
through its warehouse
of lost oars, empty nets, abandoned relics,

how it brutalizes every pebble
to polished perfection,

how it moves eternally
all things within it
to the same sea.

From the shadows

Draw shadows first
not lines, not light
everything that makes
a face its own
is in the shadows

an artist
Mother tried in vain to teach me
how to make life leap
from faces sketched
with charcoal on rough paper

down the years
I hear her words
and know them true

for never the light
of sun dappled spring
nor summer's bright bazaar
nor autumn's grace
nor winter-dazzled white
could sketch this face
I've come to wear

oh no –
it was the storm
it was the night.

Praisepoem

Praise to You by many names called,
by none defined,
Praise to You who will not be contained,
You of the limitless where
and the boundless here,
For You have filled my blood with words this day,
and play your happy songs upon my bones like a flute.
Glory be to You for the exuberance of life,
for this dance that does not cease.
Let me see You in all things created.

Glory to You for the gaudiness of flowers,
for outrageous roses never told
that pink and coral and scarlet
are not properly worn together,
for flamevine in passionate abundance
dancing in the blue and golden morning,
Glory to You for this ignorance of flowers,
for they have not been informed
that beauty commands a price,
but display their splendor
to the poorest among us who walk the field with open eyes.

Glory to You for the wonder of night sky,
for the glittering extravagance of so many stars.
Glory to You for the miracle of morning,
shattering darkness into fragments that scatter
butterflies in glad profusion
across the blossoming dawn sky.

Glory to You for this cacophony of birdsong,
For melodies of skylark and disharmonies of crow,
For plagiarizing mockingbird

and ineffable whisper of hummingbird wings.
Glory to You for all feathered flight
and also for the common caterpillar, who waking
from long sleep finds wings bejeweled
like a gift from morning:
What excess of joy bears him up,
with blossoms as his only fit companions!

Praise to You for marshland that stretches in oceanic waves
of brown and golden reeds against the sky,
How filled with Life is the tiniest drop of its water.
Glory to You for the ruby-throated lizard
and the darkness of swamp that sings with
toad and serpent and cry of heron,
with vulture and with snowy ibis,
each with a place and a beauty
that You have ordained.

Glory to You for brown and russet, for gray and indigo,
for the thousand-colored shadows
of this deepstill meditation of reed and bog,
for the treasure of reflection:
Where water stands, I find pieces of sky.

Glory to You for saltwater, fresh water,
amniotic waters of the womb of Life,
For our blood that contains the same chemistry,
documenting our heritage, our source, our family.

Glory to You for the shattering of birth,
Glory to You for the wisdom of the pain of giving life,
for it reminds us that we enter this consciousness
both heirs and indebted.

Glory to You for the magnificence of stone,
for its strong and silent singing, as it teaches us
the virtue of simply being.
Glory to You for the verdant grandeur of forest,
for the bountiful home of deer and dove,
of rabbit and fox,
for whom You provide unquestioned.

I sit upon the earth and feel Your pulse beneath me.
I sit in the limbs of trees and know
I rest in Your arms like a sleepy child.
I look to the infinite reaches of space,
and You are there, laughing down at me!
I look through a microscope into a molecule of matter,
and behold: You are there, laughing up at me!

Glory to You for all limitless things:
for sand, for stars, for the subatomic world,
For through them, we see You most truly;
In them, we see You most clearly.

Oh, Inexhaustible:
You who have no limitations,
You who scoff at boundaries,

Oh, Everlasting:
You who are,
You who have been,
You who shall be ever,

Oh, Unutterable:
Your creations in all their wonder
are but pale shadows of Your Most Holy Self
How beyond imagination,
the infinite beauty of Your Face.

Praisepoem was nominated for The Pushcart Prize in 2008.

About the Poet

Nine times nominated for The Pushcart Prize, Carla Martin-Wood is the author of the recently released *Into the Windfall Light* from The Pink Petticoat Press. She is also the author of *Flight Risk & Other Poems, Songs from the Web (encore)*, and *One flew east*, all from Fortunate Childe Publications.

She has authored seven chapbooks: *Songs from the Web* (Bitter Wine Press); *Garden of Regret* and *Redheaded Stepchild* (both Pudding House Chapbook Series); *Feed Sack Majesty, HerStory,* and *The Last Magick and Other Poems* (all Fortunate Childe Publications); and *Absinthe & Valentines* (Flutter Press).

Carla's poems have appeared in a plethora of journals and numerous anthologies in the US, England, and Ireland since 1978.

She is Copy Director of an advertising agency, and freelances book design on occasion. Carla has three magnificent granddaughters: Sarah, Erica, and Caeli Grace, in order of appearance. She was nominated for Best of the Net 2010 and 2011, and is listed in the Poets & Writers Directory at www.pw.org.

Acknowledgements

The following poems were previously published as indicated.

womanpoem, Solstice Night, Contemplation after midnight first
appeared in Songs from the Web, (Bitter Wine Press, 1986)
Beslan Fields, Garden of Regret, Blessing from Garden of Regret
(Pudding House Chapbook Series, 2009)
Ticking, Saint Sharon, Sam, Hummingbirds, Windfall from
Redheaded Stepchild (Pudding House Chapbook Series, 2009)
Grace, Taking it all back, Vespers, Waiting Room, How we are loved,
from The Last Magick (Fortunate Childe Publications, 2010)
Psalm of the Lost Lamb and *Praisepoem* first appeared in Joyful!
Sunrise first appeared in Oak Bend Review
Illumination first appeared in Flutter Poetry Journal
The child who can believe first appeared in The Lyric
Don't doubt this spring first appeared in Aura Literary Arts Review

In the poem *Illumination,* "sonofagun we'll have big fun on the bayou" is
quoted from the song *Jambalaya*, written by Hank Williams, ©Sony/ATV
Music Publishing LLC

Also by this author

Into the Windfall Light
The Pink Petticoat Press

Flight Risk & Other Poems
Fortunate Childe Publications

One flew east
Fortunate Childe Publications

Songs from the Web (encore)
Fortunate Childe Publications

Absinthe & Valentines
Flutter Press

The Last Magick
Fortunate Childe Publications

HerStory
Fortunate Childe Publications

Feed Sack Majesty
Fortunate Childe Publications

Redheaded Stepchild
Pudding House Chapbook Series

Garden of Regret
Pudding House Chapbook Series